The Traveling Book
with

Share your colored versions with us ! We love seeing your results and hearing from you we are social !

The Official FB book page, stay on top of what we have in the works !
www.facebook.com/AMVWART
The Community group, share your colored pages, meet the artists, enjoy exclusive freebies, take part in community Charity books and so much more......
www.facebook.com/groups/fansandfriendsamvwart
www.facebook.com/groups/ColorAWeirdieADay
Follow us on Twitter.... @GlobalDoodlegem
We are on Instagram too
@globaldoodlegems for instagram
...and if you are not social like that we have a blog
globaldoodlegems.wordpress.com

Copyright © 2018 Global Doodle Gems
All rights are reserved by Global Doodle Gems.
Duplication of pages for personal use are allowed. You are invited to color the pages then scan/post your coloured versions to social networks, mentioning the book title and author/artist (Global Doodle Gems).
All artwork and images are protected by copyright laws. This book or any portion thereof may not, otherwise, be reproduced and/or distributed or transmitted without the express written permission of the artist/publisher of Global Doodle Gems.
All of us from the Global Doodle Gems wish you a colortastic time and look forward to seeing your wonderful color results online !

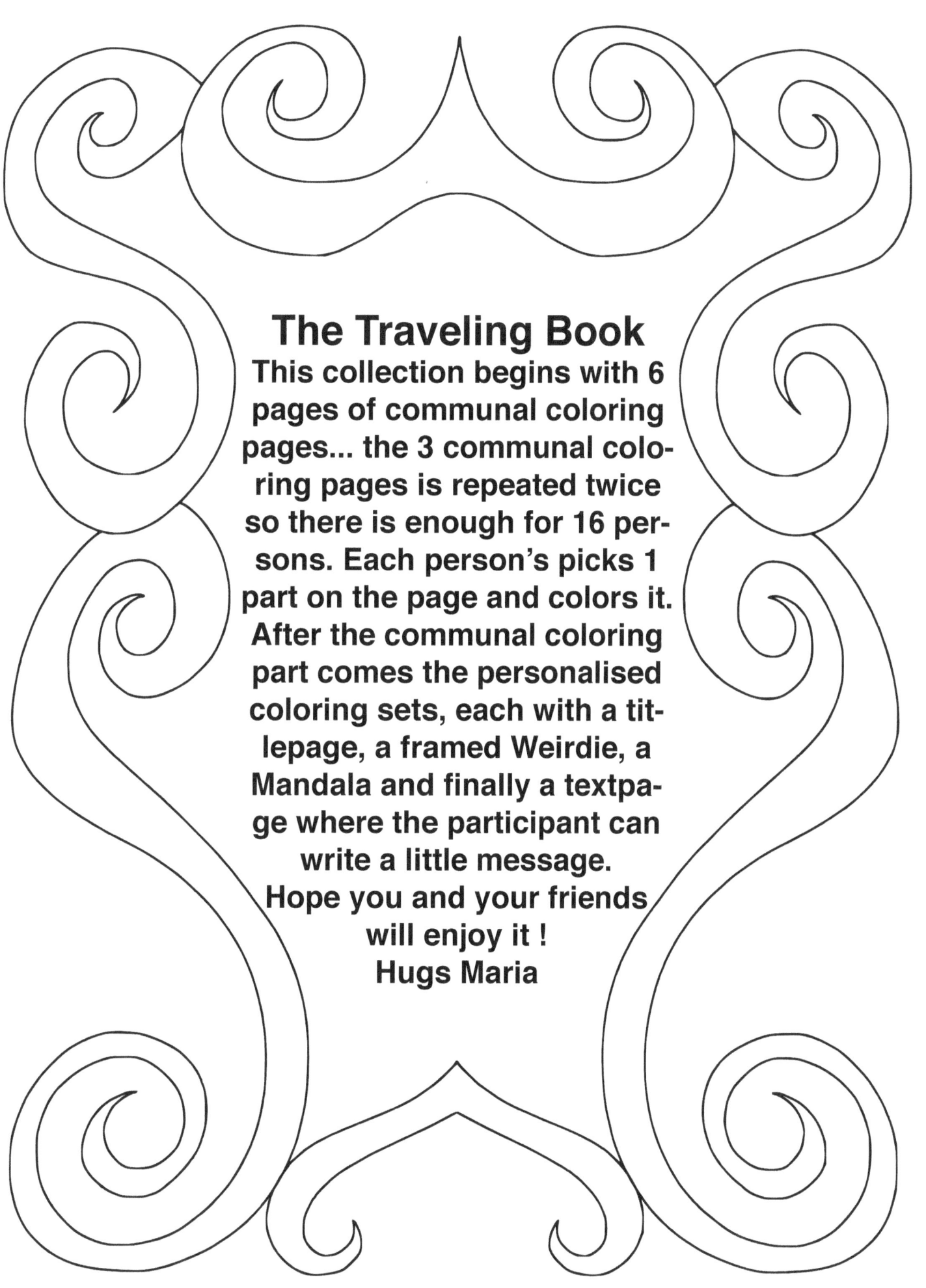

The Traveling Book

This collection begins with 6 pages of communal coloring pages... the 3 communal coloring pages is repeated twice so there is enough for 16 persons. Each person's picks 1 part on the page and colors it. After the communal coloring part comes the personalised coloring sets, each with a titlepage, a framed Weirdie, a Mandala and finally a textpage where the participant can write a little message.
Hope you and your friends will enjoy it !
Hugs Maria

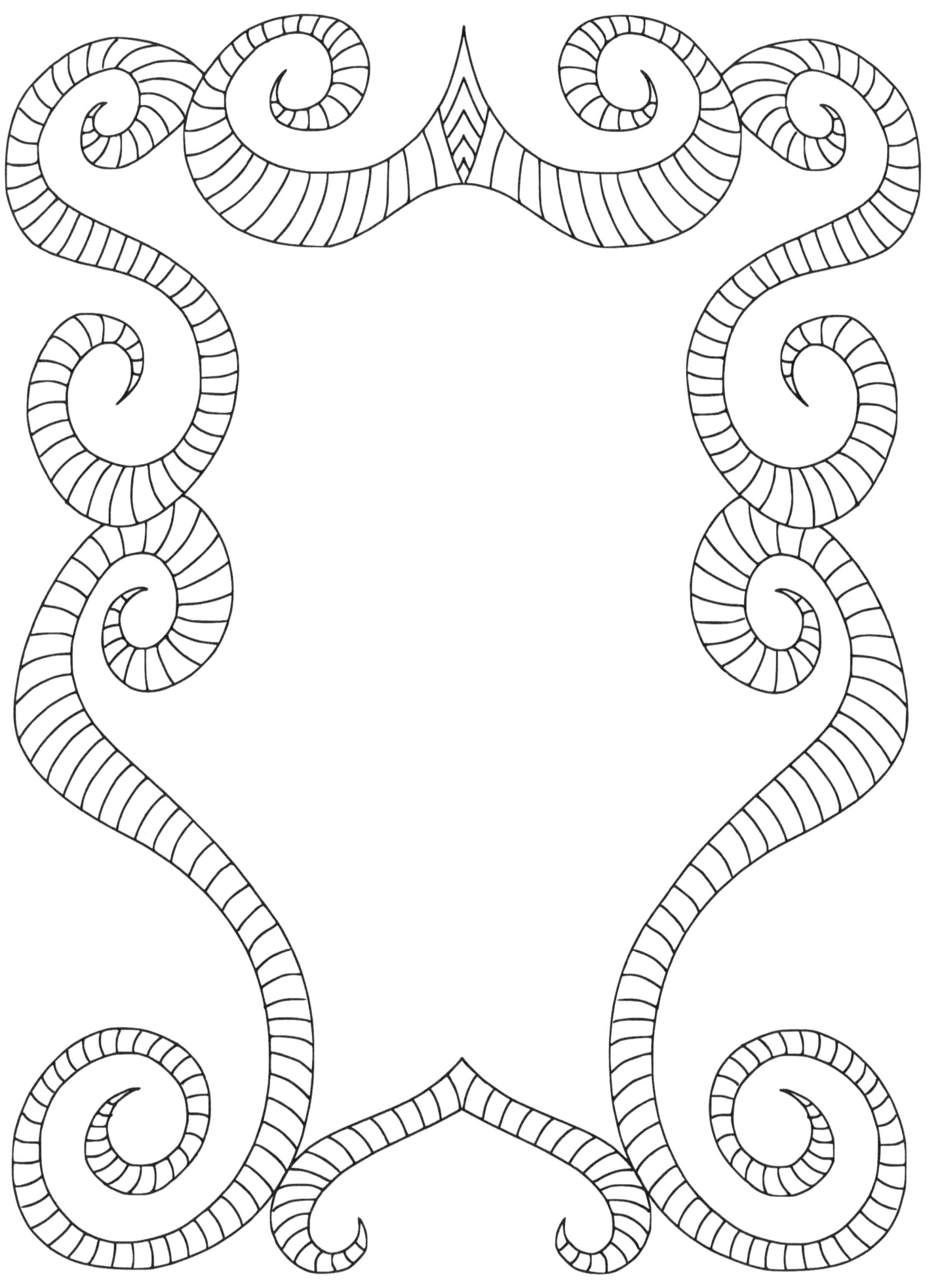

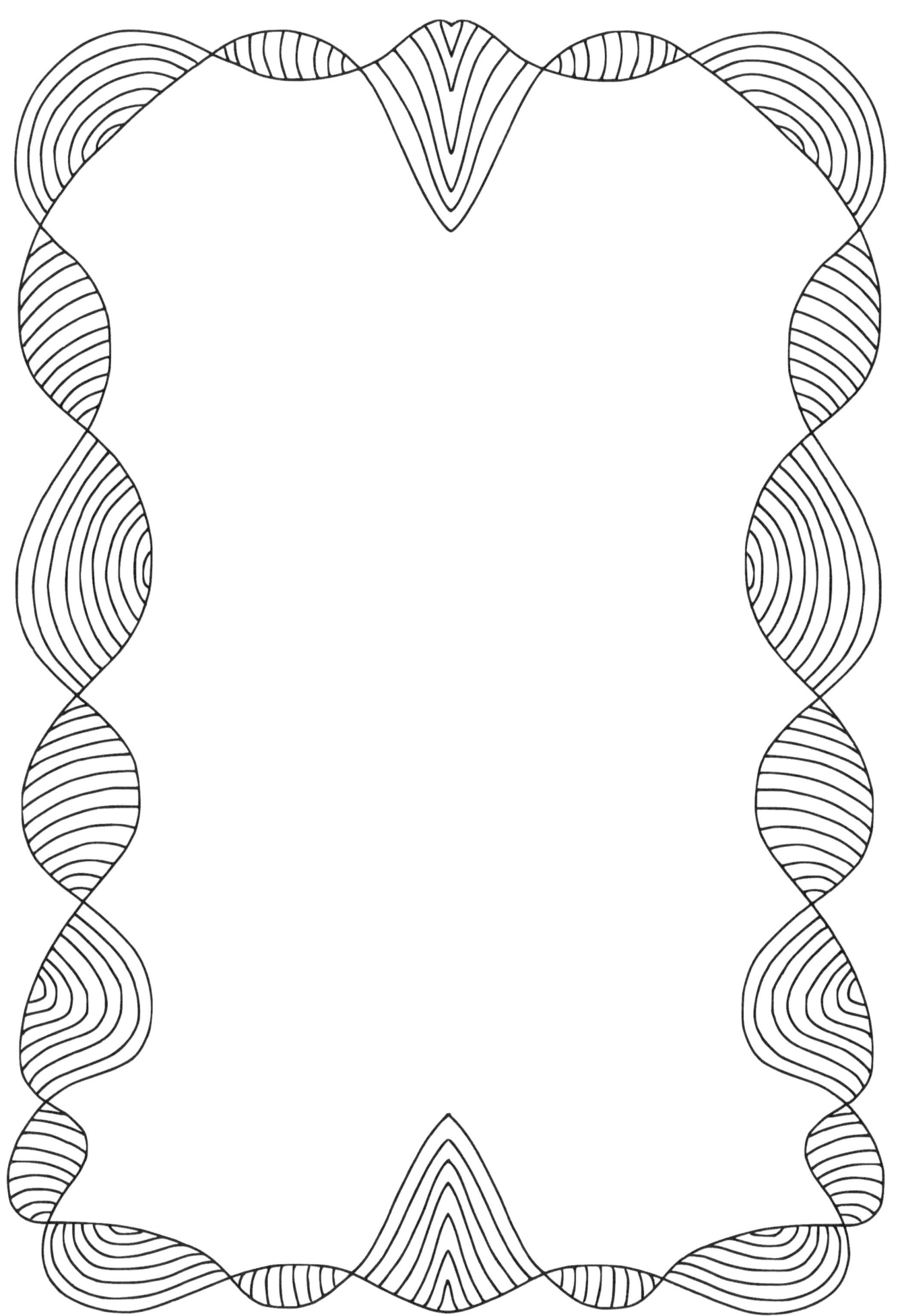

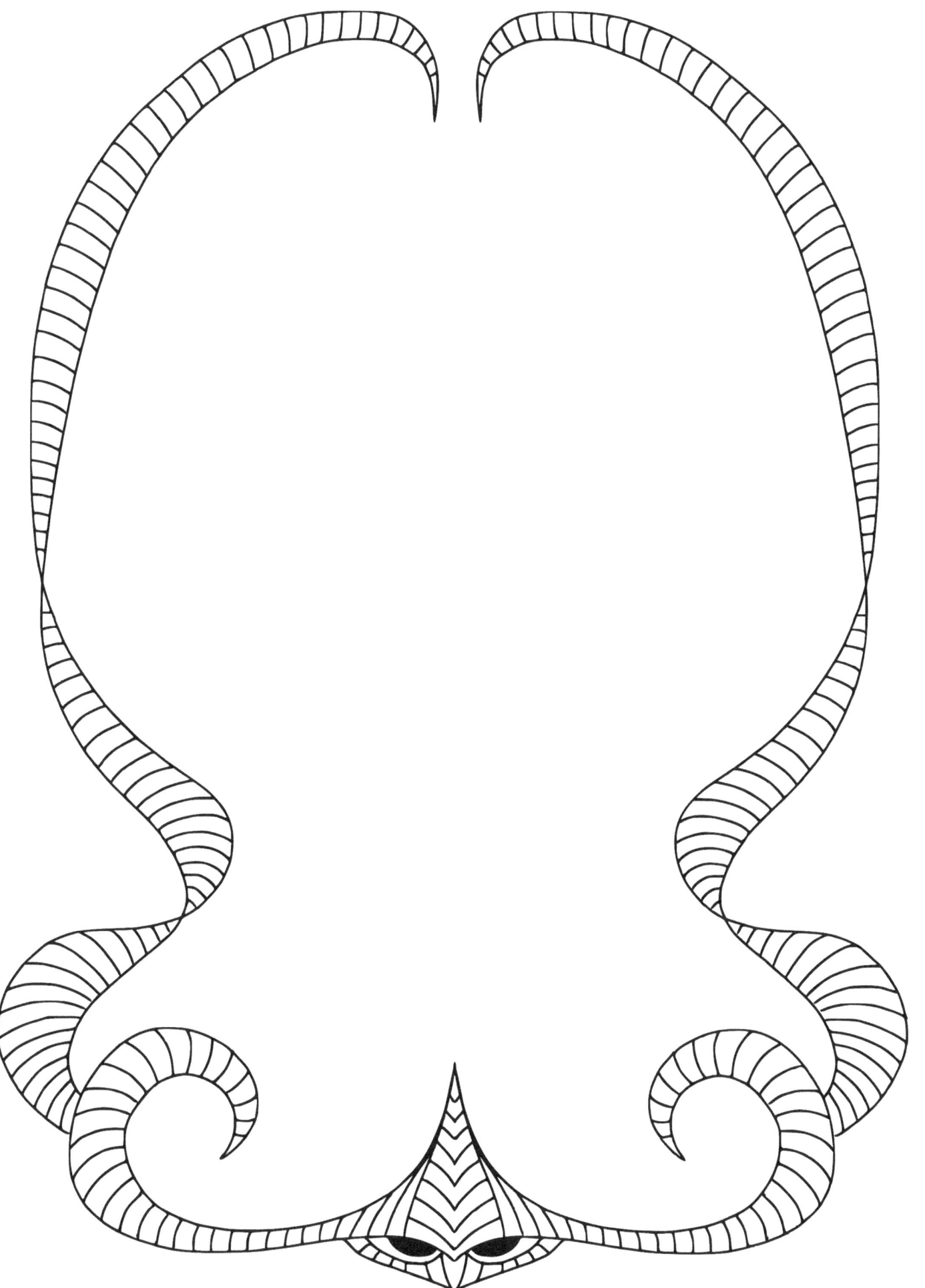

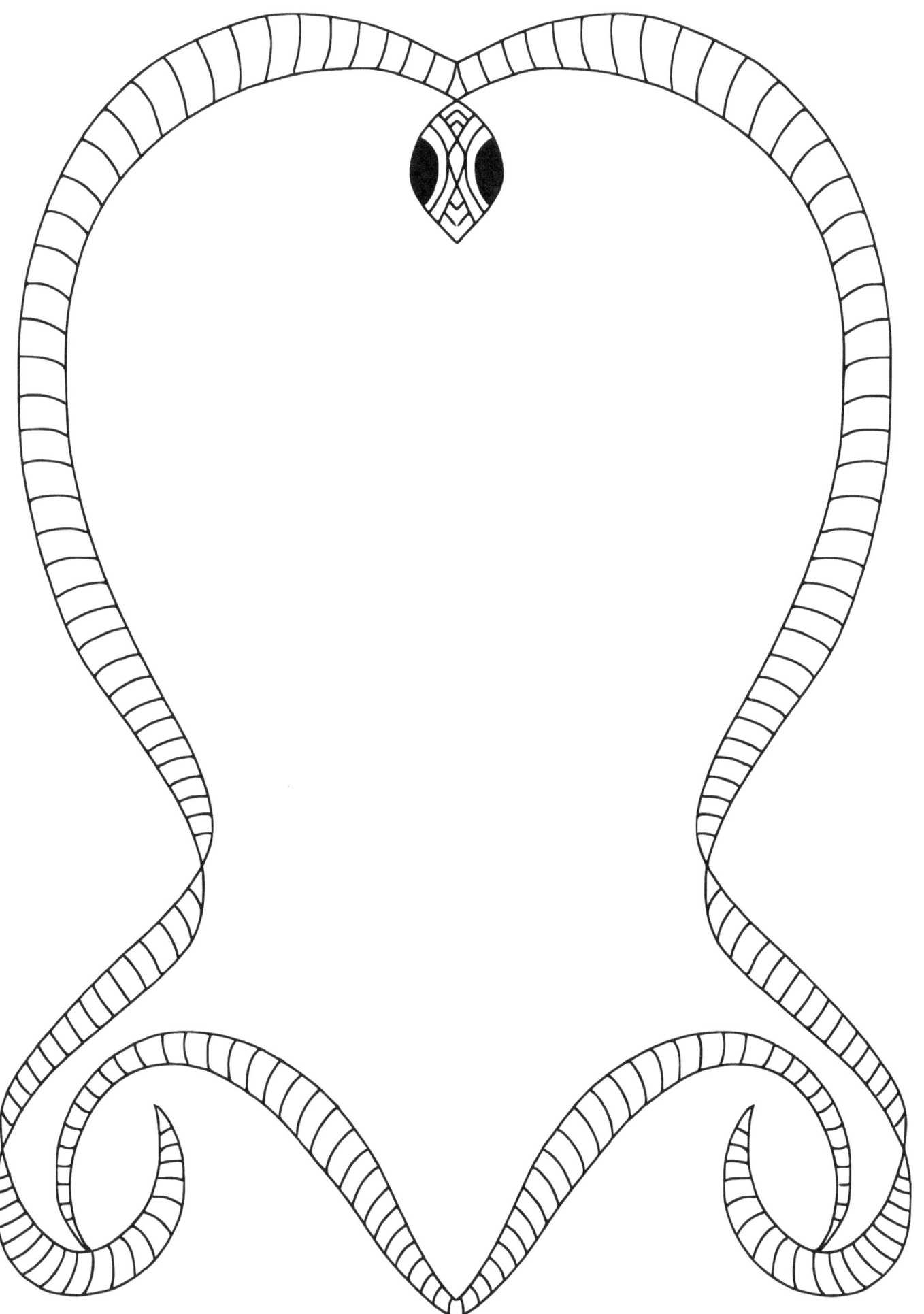

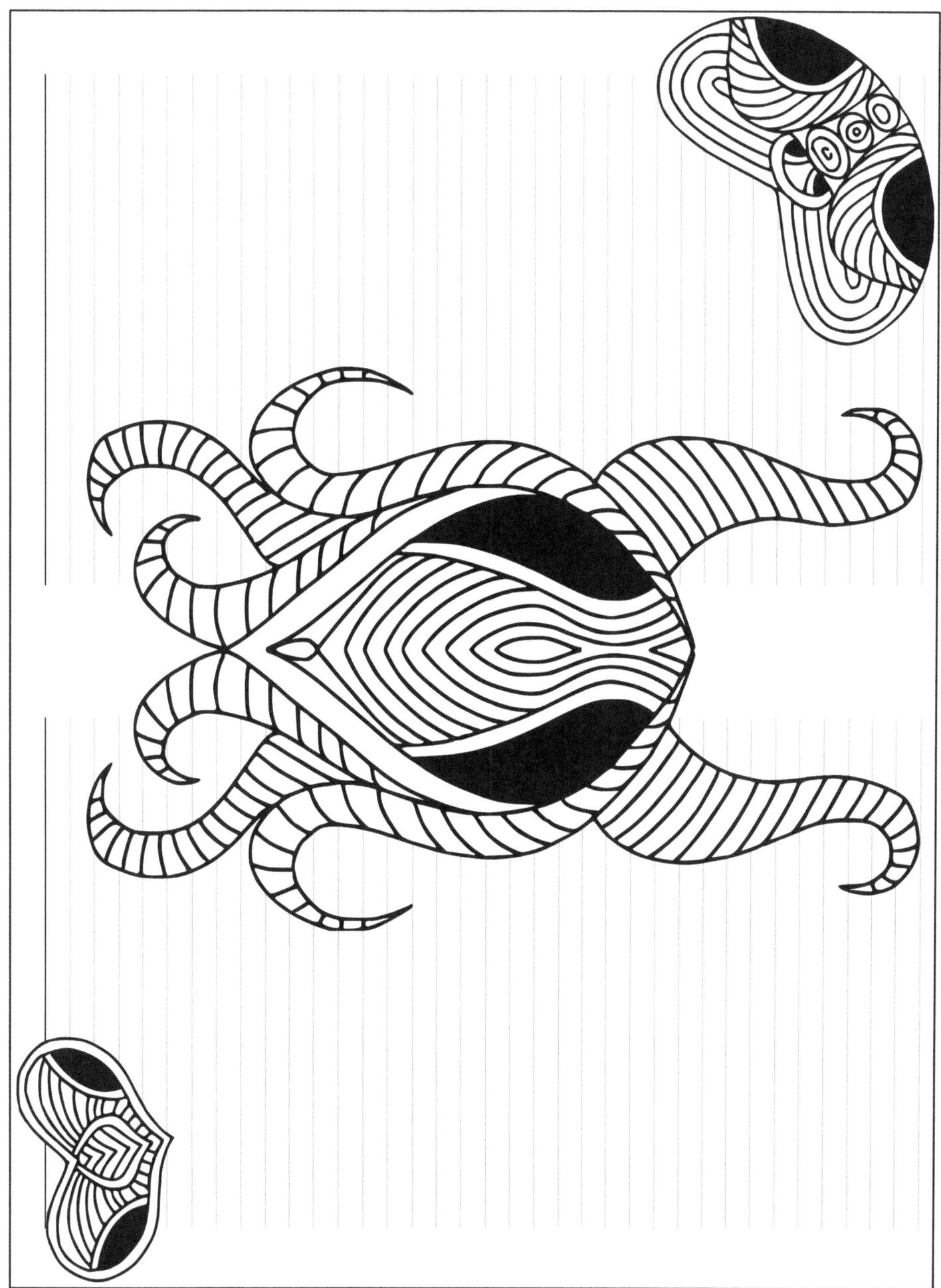

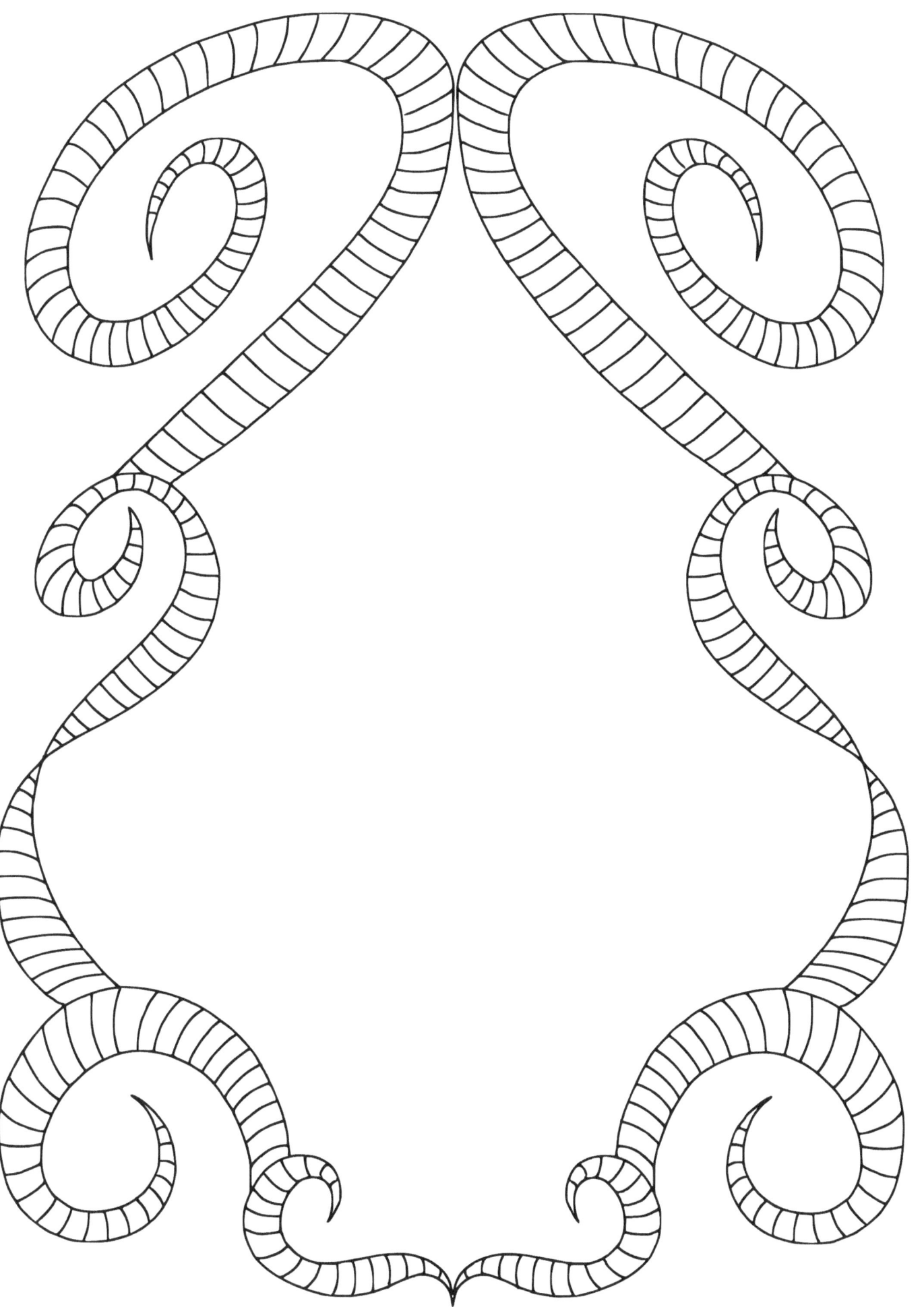

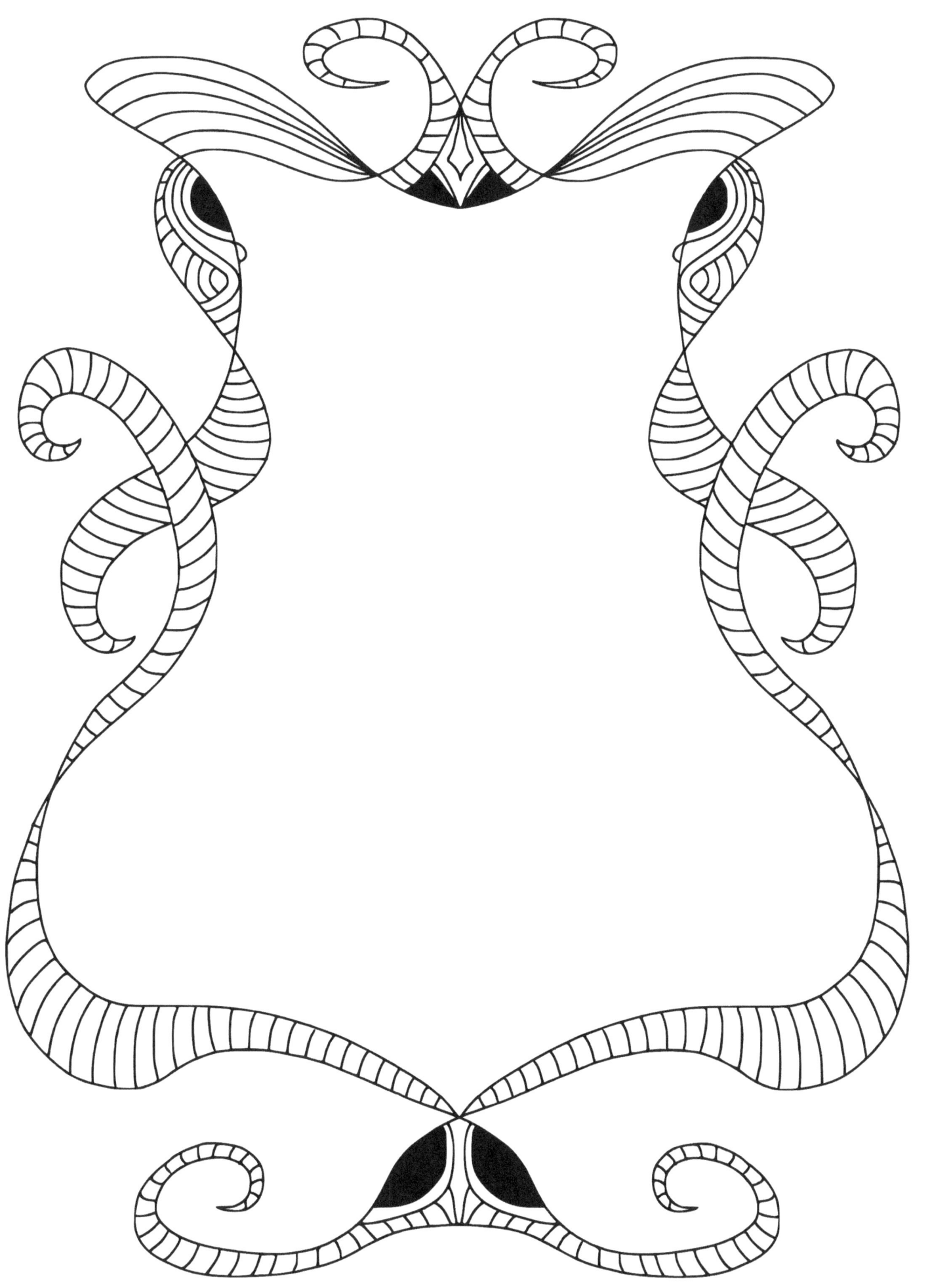

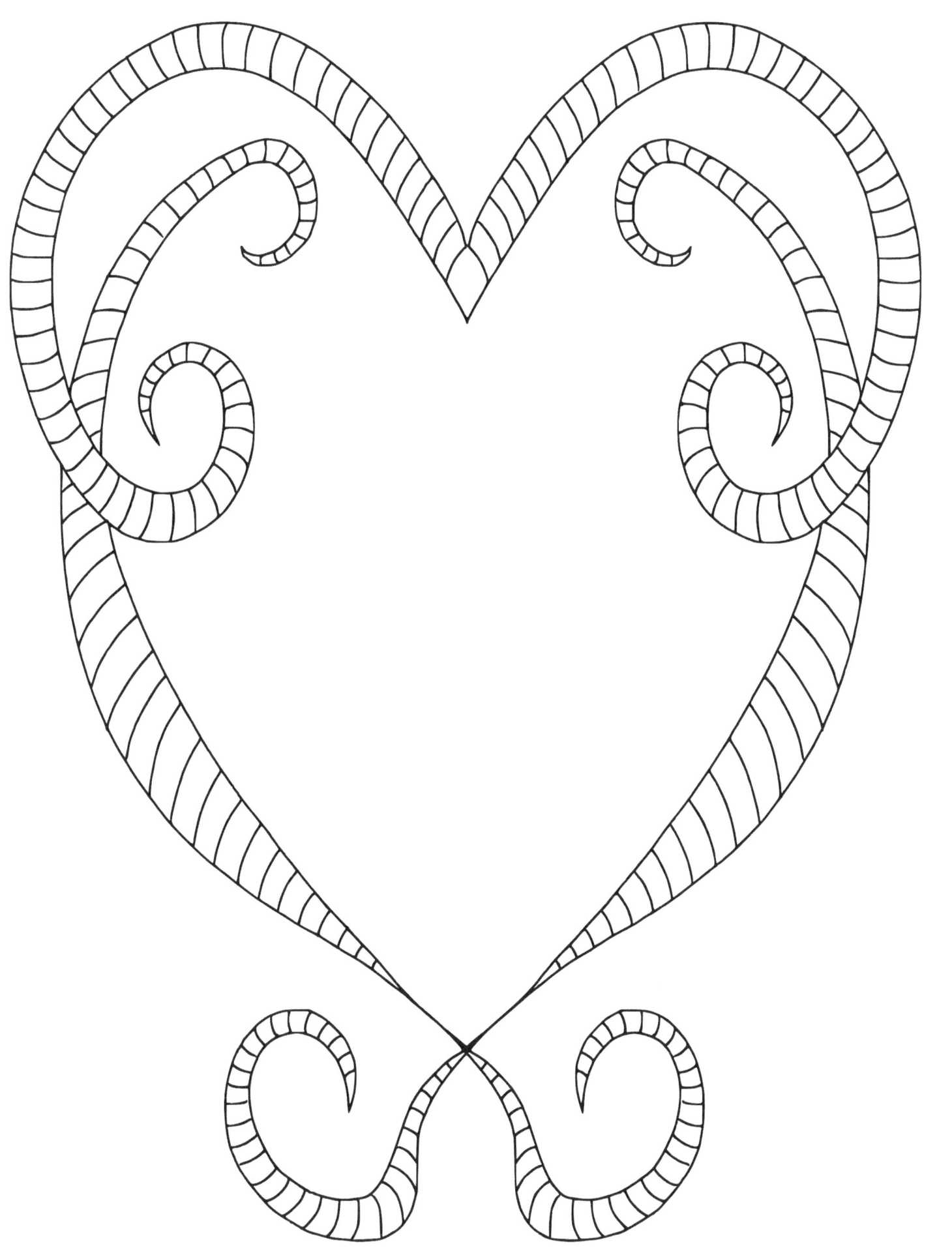

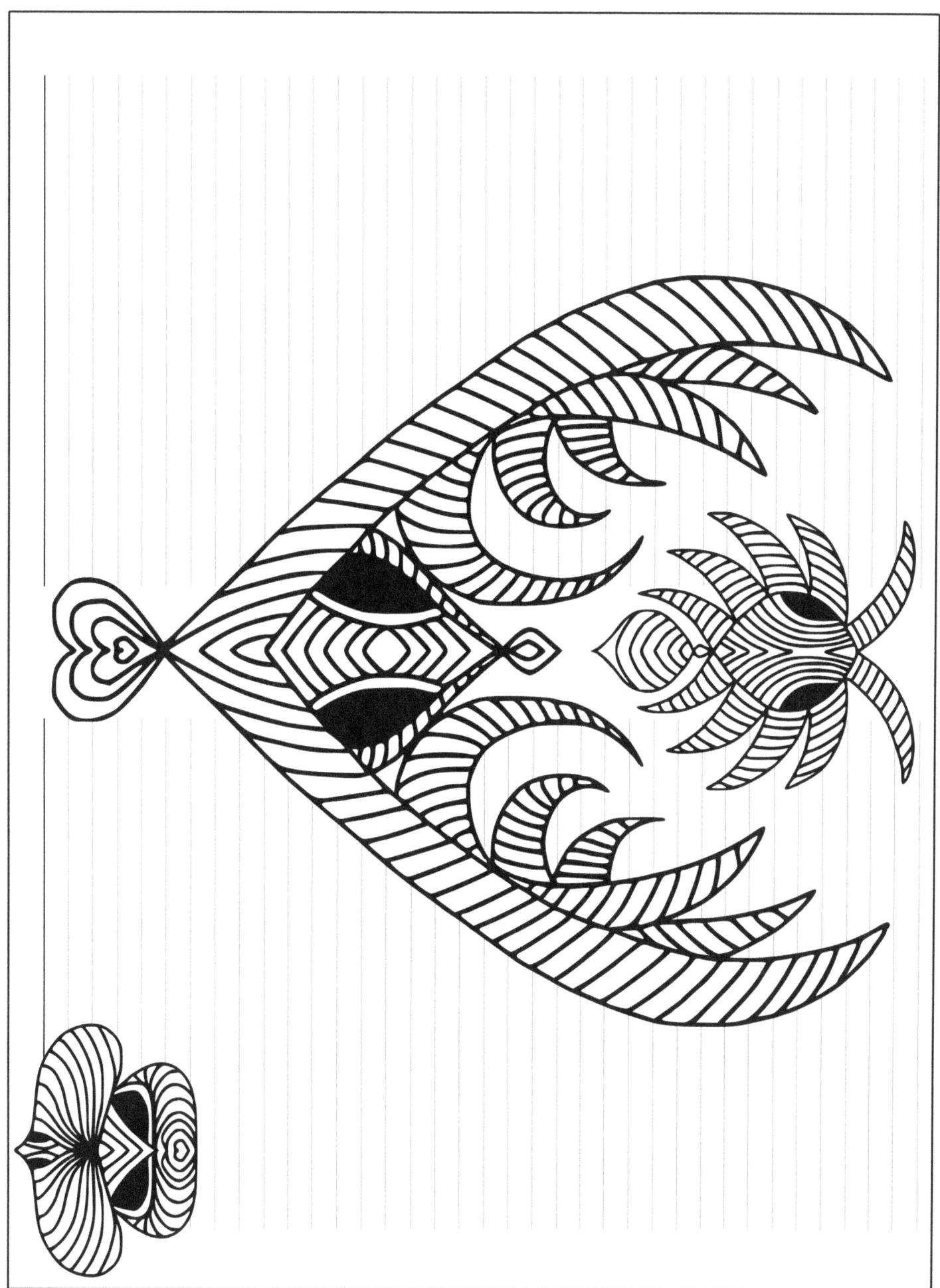

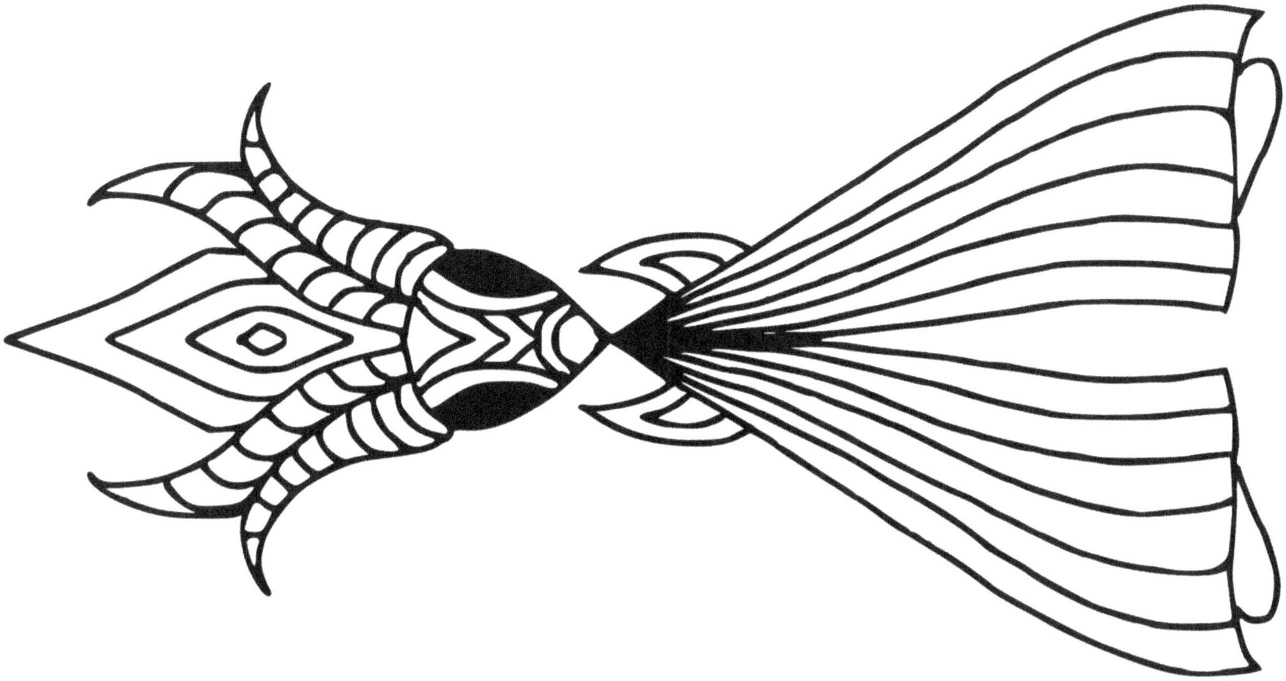

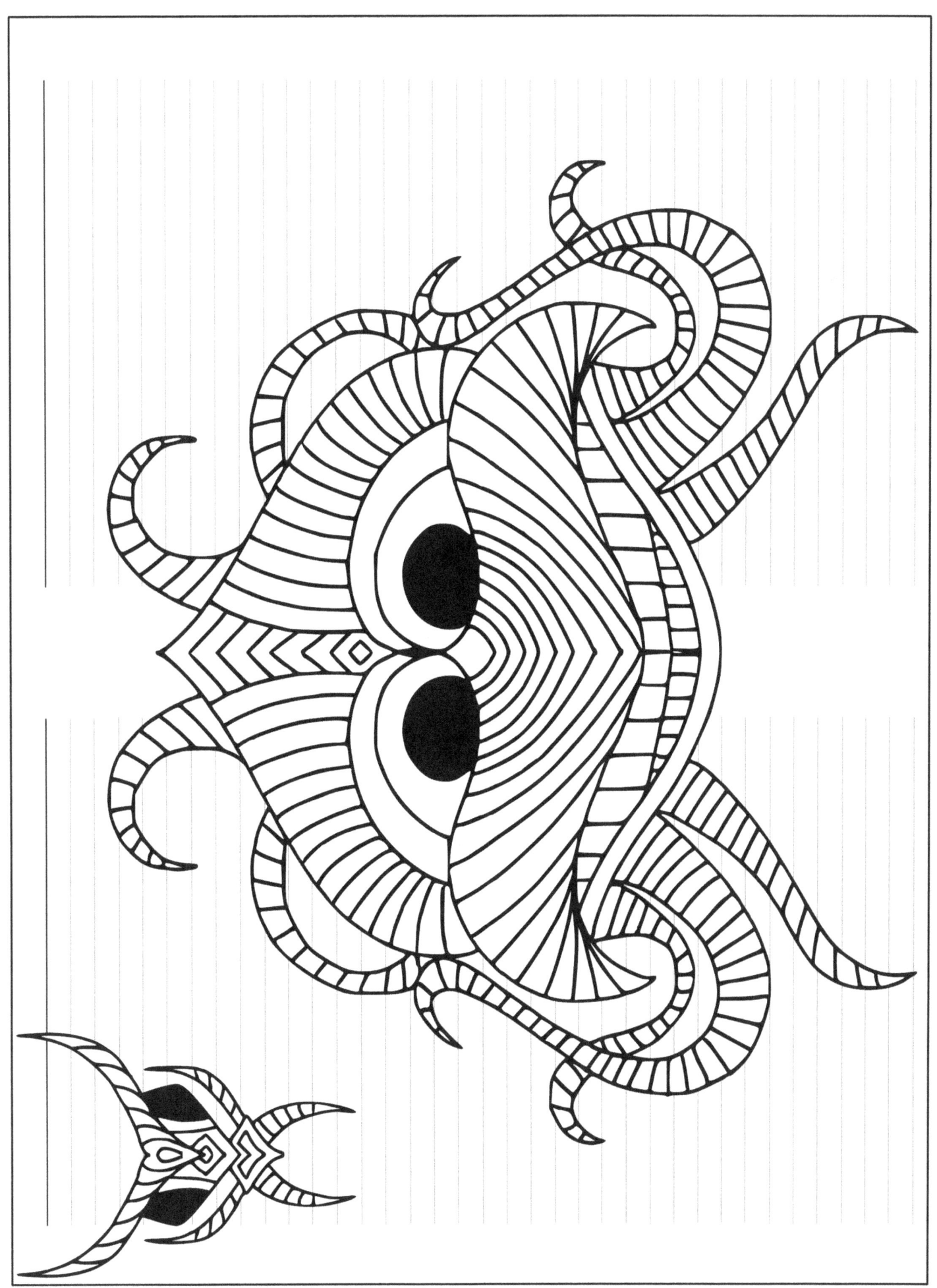